MILITARY SPECIAL OPS

NAVY SEALS

ELITE OPERATIONS

BY PATRICIA NEWMAN

Lerner Publications Company
Minneapolis

Lerner Publications Company
A division of Lerner Publishing Group, Inc.
241 First Avenue North
Minneapolis, MN 55401 U.S.A.

Website address: www.lernerbooks.com

Content Consultant: Kalev Sepp, assistant professor, Naval Postgraduate
School

Library of Congress Cataloging-in-Publication Data
Newman, Patricia.
    Navy SEALs : elite operations / by Patricia Newman.
      pages   cm. — (Military special ops)
    Includes index.
    ISBN 978-0-7613-9080-0 (lib. bdg. : alk. paper)
    ISBN 978-1-4677-1766-3 (eBook)
    1. United States. Navy. SEALs—Juvenile literature. 2. United States.
  Navy—Commando troops—Juvenile literature. I. Title.
  VG87N48 2014
  359.9'84—dc23   2013001738

Manufactured in the United States of America
1 — MG — 7/15/13

The images in this book are used with the permission of: © Aleksandar
Mijatovic/Shutterstock Images, backgrounds; Michael J. Pusnik, Jr./U.S.
Navy, 5; U.S. Navy, 6, 10, 11, 14–15, 17, 18, 21, 26, 29; © AP Images,
8; Anthony Harding/U.S. Navy, 13; Ryan Rholes/U.S. Marine Corps, 19;
Andrew McKaskle/U.S. Navy, 20; Arcenio Gonzalez Jr./U.S. Navy, 23;
John DeCoursey/U.S. Navy, 24; Michelle Kapica/U.S. Navy, 25, 28; Kyle
D. Gahlau/U.S. Navy, 27.

Front cover: U.S. Naval Special Warfare Command.

Main body text set in Tw Cen MT Std Medium 12/18.
Typeface provided by Adobe Systems.

CONTENTS

CHAPTER ONE: PUBLIC ENEMY NUMBER ONE

It was May 2, 2011: go day. A team of U.S. Navy SEALs sat in the pitch-dark helicopter as it flew through the night to their objective. The roar of the engines made talking without headset radios impossible. The team adjusted their helmets and checked their radios and weapons. They were ready to toss ropes out of the chopper and slide down to the ground inside a walled courtyard by a house. The target: Osama

MISSION IN FOCUS

WHAT HAPPENED ON SEPTEMBER 11, 2001?

Osama bin Laden was behind a deadly attack on American soil. Al-Qaeda terrorists hijacked American Airlines Flight 11 and United Airlines Flight 175. The terrorists broke into the cockpits, took over the planes, and flew them into the twin towers of the World Trade Center. The crashes killed everyone on board and destroyed the 110-story buildings. Thirty-three minutes later, American Airlines Flight 77 crashed into the Pentagon near Washington, D.C. A fourth plane was hijacked, United Airlines Flight 93, possibly to crash into the White House. Heroic passengers attacked the hijackers. The terrorists lost control, and the plane crashed in a field in Pennsylvania instead. Altogether, nearly three thousand people died that day in the attacks.

SEALs fast-rope onto the deck of an aircraft carrier.

bin Laden—public enemy number one. The man responsible for killing nearly three thousand Americans on September 11, 2001.

However, something was wrong. The chopper could not hover. It lurched around in the air over the courtyard. Then it began to fall to the ground. The chopper was going to crash. "This is going to hurt," thought one team member.

The helicopter crashed nose first in an open yard inside bin Laden's compound. Thanks to the skill of the pilot, nobody was hurt. However, the team had lost the element of surprise. The SEALs leaped out of the chopper. They would complete their mission no matter what.

Two groups of SEALs rushed into the two houses in the compound. One group overcame several members of bin Laden's terrorist organization, al-Qaeda. Two SEALs guarded the outside of the compound with a combat assault dog.

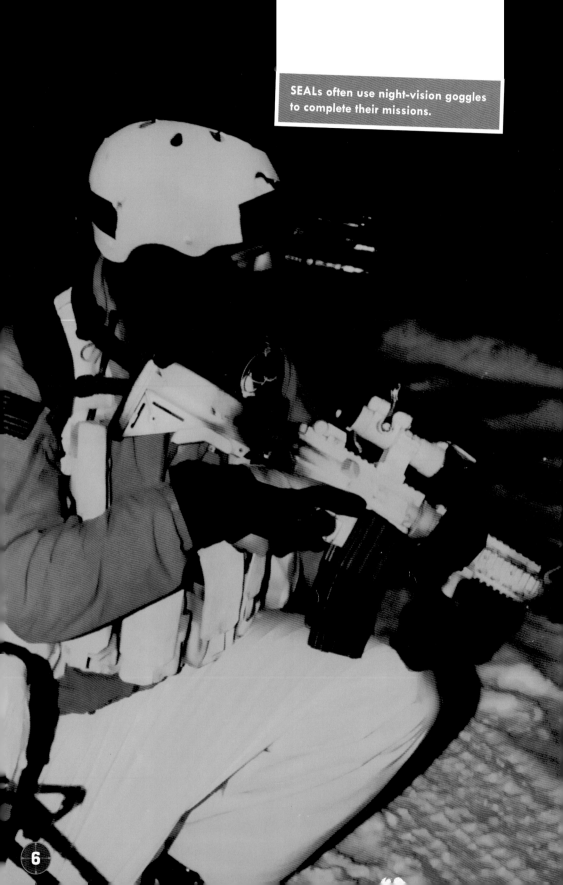

SEALs often use night-vision goggles to complete their missions.

Another assault team crept up the dark stairs to bin Laden's apartment on the third floor. Night-vision goggles turned the world green. The SEALs did not talk, run, or yell. "Think quiet," one team member reminded himself. His ears strained to hear the sound of enemy footsteps.

On the top step, one SEAL saw a person's head poking out of one of the doorways. The SEAL fired. The person fell back into the dark room. The SEALs approached slowly. Inside, two women wailed. A man in a tunic, white T-shirt, and tan pants lay sprawled on the floor, dead. But was it Osama bin Laden? The SEAL team secured the compound. Then the SEALs took saliva samples to identify the man. They took photos and collected notebooks, computer drives, and videos. Since bin Laden was very tall, they even measured the man. Finally, they called their commander at their home base. They gave the code words: "Geronimo EKIA." This meant, "Osama bin Laden, enemy killed in action."

Failure is not an option for Navy SEALs. They work in any environment. SEAL stands for <u>se</u>a, <u>a</u>ir, <u>l</u>and. SEALs can operate under extreme conditions with little food and less sleep. Every mission tests their courage and skill. Navy SEALs are respected as among the very best of the U.S. military's Special Operations Forces.

SEAL TEAM SIX

The Navy SEALs who carried out the raid on bin Laden were members of SEAL Team Six. For reasons of secrecy, the team was called the U.S. Naval Special Warfare Development Group (DEVGRU). The missions of this elite group are highly secret. Much of their work is preventing terrorism or catching terrorists. They also rescue hostages and protect world leaders from assassins. Only the best SEALs are eligible for DEVGRU.

CHAPTER TWO:
SEAL PIONEERS

Before there were SEALs, there were underwater demolition teams (UDTs) known as frogmen. UDTs operated during World War II (1939–1945) and the Korean War (1950–1953). UDTs wore swimsuits, fins, and masks. They were some of the first swimmers to use scuba gear. They swam ahead of beach landings in World War II. They cleared away obstacles so landing craft carrying marines and soldiers could get to the beach. UDTs went ashore and destroyed railroads,

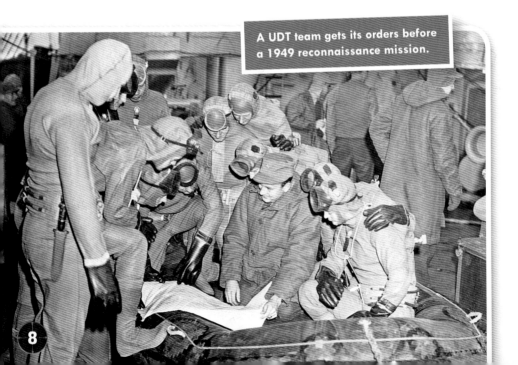

A UDT team gets its orders before a 1949 reconnaissance mission.

MEDAL OF HONOR RECIPIENTS

Three SEALs received the Medal of Honor for their service during the Vietnam War (1957–1975). Lieutenant Thomas R. Norris disguised himself as a fisherman and crossed enemy territory to rescue a downed pilot.

Michael E. Thornton, petty officer second class, was gathering intelligence in enemy territory. His commanding officer for the mission was Lieutenant Norris. This was only months after Norris's own Medal of Honor action. Norris was seriously wounded. Thornton ran back into enemy fire to rescue Norris.

Lieutenant Joseph R. Kerrey led a mission to capture enemy leaders. He led his team down a 350-foot (107-meter) cliff. Seriously injured by a grenade explosion, he continued to direct his men. They successfully completed the mission. Kerrey was rescued by helicopter.

tunnels, and bridges behind enemy lines in Korea. They also scouted the shorelines for land mines.

In the early 1960s, President John F. Kennedy called for soldiers, sailors, airmen, and marines skilled in unconventional warfare tactics. In January 1962, SEAL Teams One and Two were established. The new SEALs were mostly former UDT members. In February 1966, SEAL Team One was deployed into combat in Vietnam. The team's special skills in unconventional warfare gave it an advantage over the enemy.

In 1980 anti-American radicals took fifty-two Americans hostage in the U.S. Embassy in Tehran, Iran. President Jimmy Carter ordered the U.S. military to rescue them. Unfortunately, this mission, code-named Operation Eagle Claw, failed.

Many SEAL missions require stealth and secrecy.

The U.S. military realized it needed more counterterrorist units. The U.S. Navy designated SEAL Team Six for this mission, calling the unit the U.S. Naval Special Warfare Development Group. DEVGRU is the Navy's specialized counterterrorism unit. Today, one of DEVGRU's chief tasks is to hunt down and capture or kill terrorists.

After the terrorist attacks of September 11, 2001, the United States increased counterterrorist actions in Asia and the Middle East. In Afghanistan, SEALs hunted terrorists and the leaders of the Taliban, an extremist group that imposed strict religious law on the country. In Iraq, SEALs guarded oil wells and refineries against terrorist attacks. They cleared the rivers and the harbors so food and medicine could be sent to Iraqi citizens.

SEAL teams are deployed on important missions around the world every day. SEAL operations fall into four categories.

1. Direct action missions. These include raids and ambushes against enemy targets.

2. Special reconnaissance, or "recon," missions. These send SEAL teams into enemy territory. The teams monitor and report on enemy activity. The teams gather information about beach and water conditions before a beach landing. The military uses recon to help plan future missions.

3. Counterterrorism missions. These search out terrorist groups and try to prevent terrorist attacks.

4. Foreign internal defense missions. These require SEALs to train U.S. allies overseas to overcome enemy threats on their own.

SEALs are experts in amphibious operations.

CHAPTER THREE:
BY SEA, BY AIR, BY LAND

SEALs approach the enemy from sea, air, or land. SEALs use many different skills to complete their missions. They might use explosives to blow open the doors of an enemy hideout. SEALs might sneak up on sleeping enemies to catch them off guard. SEALs can chase down pirates at sea. And SEALs can rescue hostages held by terrorists.

At sea, SEAL scouts are usually the first to land on a beach ahead of a landing force of marines and soldiers. SEALs evaluate the danger

MISSION IN FOCUS   RESCUING JESSICA

Jessica Buchanan was an aid worker in Somalia who educated the poor. In 2011 Somali bandits kidnapped her and one of her coworkers. The bandits wanted $10 million in ransom money to set her free. Talks with the bandits had failed, and Buchanan was ill. President Barack Obama ordered a SEAL team to raid the bandits' camp and rescue the two aid workers. The SEALs parachuted from a plane under cover of darkness. They landed within a few miles of the hideout and hiked the rest of the way. The poorly trained bandits did not have a chance against an elite strike force, and the rescue was successful.

SEALs parachute from a C-130 Hercules aircraft as part of their training.

before signaling the main force to land. By air, SEALs can ride a chopper into enemy territory and fast-rope to the ground. They can also parachute from cargo planes flying high above their objective. Then SEALs glide silently to their target with steerable parachutes. On land, SEALs often travel on foot. They might scale a cliff and creep along a goat path for a recon mission.

In some missions, SEALs combine sea, air, and land tactics. For instance, SEALs can attach a parachute to a boat equipped for a beach assault. Flying over the ocean in a cargo plane at night, they push the boat out the back of the plane. Then they follow it, one after another, parachuting into the sea. Then they abandon their parachutes, swim to their boat, start its motor, and ride it to the beach. Once ashore, they move over land to their target. They hope to surprise the enemy by coming at it from an unexpected direction.

Each SEAL team has up to ten SEAL platoons. A SEAL platoon has two officers and fourteen enlisted sailors. If necessary, the team can split into two squads of one officer and seven sailors each. Sometimes for ambushes or raids, a squad can split into two "fire teams" of four men each. The squads and fire teams are fast and agile. Because of their small size, they are hard for an enemy to detect.

Since they were established in 1962, SEAL teams have played an active role in conflicts around the globe. In 2003 the United States invaded Iraq to remove the dictator Saddam Hussein, who was threatening to attack his neighbors with missiles. U.S. commanders believed he planned to destroy a dam. This would flood the roads and bridges downstream and slow down the U.S. advance. SEALs joined with a special forces unit from Poland to save the dam from destruction.

SEALs usually work in small teams.

Pirates based along the shore of Somalia tried to capture the cargo ship *Maersk Alabama* in April 2009. SEALs parachuted into the ocean, where they were picked up by U.S. Navy warships. The pirates were surrounded. They threatened to kill the ship's captain unless they were allowed to go back to shore. At dusk three SEAL snipers using night-vision scopes zeroed in on the pirates. They saw a pirate pointing a gun at the captain. The three SEALs fired, and three pirates fell dead. The SEALs boarded the lifeboat and rescued the captain.

"The greatest compliment one SEAL can bestow on another is to call him a teammate."

—Admiral William McRaven, head of U.S. Special Operations Command and a SEAL

CHAPTER FOUR:
THE SEAL KIT

SEALs choose their uniforms depending on the weather and their mission. For land missions, SEALs often wear camouflage shirts and pants. The pattern of the camouflage depends on the environment of the mission. Forest settings require a green, brown, and black pattern. Six patterns are available for desert missions. The SEALs' choice depends on the color of the ground cover. This varies from desert to desert on different continents. Two city patterns match either light-colored buildings or dark buildings and shadows. Cold weather requires heavy boots, warm pants, and parkas.

SEALs use the term *kit* for their gear and equipment. To help them carry what they need, SEALs have a vest with many pockets. They store fresh batteries in one pocket. Leather gloves for fast-roping are in another. Grenades are in yet another. Heavy bulletproof plates fit in large pouches. The plates shield SEALs from gunfire. Bolt cutters to cut padlocks on doors might be strapped to a SEAL's back. Night-vision goggles are mounted to their helmets.

"We demand discipline. We expect innovation. The lives of my teammates and the success of the mission depend on me—my technical skill, tactical proficiency, and attention to detail. My training is never complete."

—Navy SEAL Code excerpt

Their clothing and kits allow SEALs to operate in all kinds of weather and terrain.

High-tech equipment includes sophisticated binoculars and cameras.

Combat assault dogs are an asset on many missions.

Team members choose from a variety of weapons depending on the mission. Assault rifles, submachine guns, and pistols are often the usual choices. Some of the guns have suppressors to quiet the sound of the gunfire. Some missions require a specially trained combat assault dog. The dog tracks down enemies who try to hide from the SEALs. A dog can also sniff out enemy booby traps.

Before every mission, SEALs double-check the batteries in their night-vision goggles and the laser sights on their guns. They check their radios to make sure everyone is on the correct frequency. The DEVGRU SEALs also use bone phones. These special communication devices sit on their cheeks. The men can hear radio traffic through vibrations in their cheekbones that travel to the small bones in their ears. Bone phones are extremely quiet. No one can overhear a conversation. Since there are no earbuds, others don't even know the SEAL is using a radio.

Missions at sea require different gear. Dive suits keep SEALs warm in freezing water. Depending on the mission, SEALs choose between two types of underwater breathing devices. The first is the scuba system. This has an air tank and a hose from which the SEALs breathe. Bubbles float to the surface as the swimmers breathe out. This is called an open system.

When SEALs ride a SEAL Delivery Vehicle (SDV), they use their scuba gear to breathe.

If secrecy is important, then SEALs choose a closed system. There are no bubbles to give away the swimmers' locations. The closed system recycles each breath. It cleans the swimmers' exhaled carbon dioxide and adds oxygen.

SEALs use a variety of boats for their missions. One of the most popular is an inflatable raft. It has several names, including the Combat Rubber Raiding Raft, or the Zodiac, which is named after the company that makes it. These boats are nicknamed rubber ducks. The SEAL Delivery Vehicle (SDV) is a small submarine that carries only a couple of people. Passengers are exposed to the water. The SDV transports SEALs underwater, helping keep their missions secret.

To reach their target, SEALs might push their Zodiac out of an airplane and jump into the ocean after it. Sometimes they fast-rope to the ground from a hovering helicopter. Team members might also parachute from a high altitude for more secrecy. The SEALs open their chutes high in the air. They glide silently to their drop zone. During these high-altitude jumps, the SEALs breathe from oxygen tanks. The air keeps them from passing out.

SEALS IN FLIGHT

SEALs fly in long-range cargo planes to reach missions far from home. Military cargo planes do not have many luxuries. During a long flight, some men might sleep on top of equipment boxes. Some find a sliver of space on the floor of the cargo bay of the plane. Others might bring air mattresses or hammocks to grab some shut-eye.

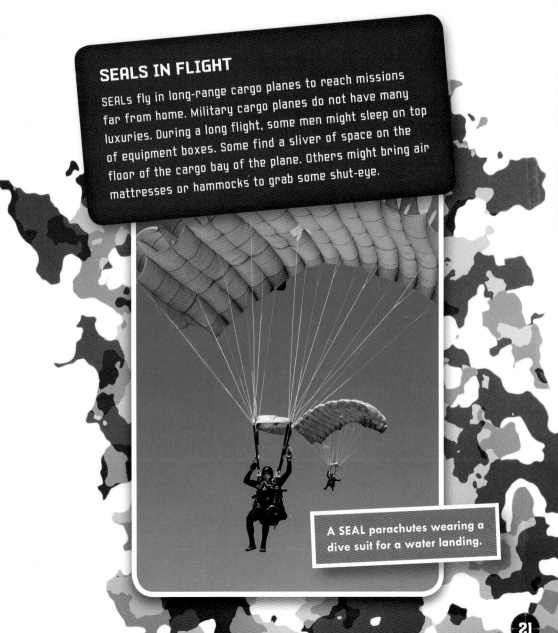

A SEAL parachutes wearing a dive suit for a water landing.

CHAPTER FIVE: EARNING THE TRIDENT

U.S. Navy men ages seventeen to twenty-eight may apply to become SEALs. They must be highly recommended by their commanding officers. Servicemen from other branches of the military may also apply. All candidates must score high on written exams and physical fitness tests.

PHYSICAL FITNESS

Incoming SEAL candidates must be able to perform the following by the end of the preparation class:

★ Swim 1,000 yards (914 m) with swim fins in less than twenty minutes

★ Complete seventy push-ups in two minutes

★ Complete sixty sit-ups in two minutes

★ Do at least ten pull-ups

★ Run 4 miles (6.4 kilometers) in combat uniform and boots in less than thirty-one minutes.

A SEAL candidate goes down a rope in a training exercise. SEALs must conquer any fear of heights.

First, candidates attend a preparation class in Great Lakes, Illinois. This two-month class tests their mental and physical toughness. Candidates who cannot meet the tough standards return to other important jobs in the military. Candidates who pass move to Coronado, California. They attend Basic Underwater Demolition/SEAL orientation class, called BUD/S for short. The three-week orientation teaches candidates their way around the Naval Special Warfare Center. Instructors introduce the candidates to the BUD/S physical training program and the obstacle course. These three weeks prepare the candidates for day one of First Phase.

SEAL candidates train in cold water to test how they handle stress.

The seven weeks of First Phase include physical training on land and in the water. Groups of five or six men run up sand dunes carrying a log weighing 400 to 600 pounds (180 to 270 kilograms). They are on the run all day long. They do sit-ups holding a rubber raft over their heads. Candidates have to hold their breath underwater for at least two minutes. They are taught to swim with their hands and feet tied. Slow candidates get the "sugar cookie" treatment. They have to dive in the surf and then roll on the beach to cover themselves with sand, like a sugar cookie, before returning to their group to try harder.

SEAL candidates perform buddy carries, improving their strength and endurance.

"The only easy day was yesterday."
—The wooden sign at the SEAL training base in California

Week four of First Phase is called Hell Week. According to one instructor, Hell Week "begins with a bang." Explosions. Gunfire. Flares. Smoke. The instructors try to create confusion among the candidates. Potential SEALs must demonstrate their mental toughness.

Candidates run a total of 200 miles (320 km) during the week, do exercises and workouts for twenty hours a day, and sleep a total of four hours during the five-and-one-half-day stretch. Hell Week measures the "heart" of each man—his will to succeed in the face of extreme stress.

Practice in swimming, diving, and combat maneuvers is essential for SEAL candidates.

In the weeks that follow, candidates get more sleep and food, but they continue to swim, run, and exercise constantly. A brass bell waits for those who cannot endure the demanding training. Any candidate may drop out of training by ringing the bell three times. He will return to regular duty. The candidates who succeed are those who decide that quitting is not an option.

Second Phase trains the candidates in combat diving skills. This phase lasts seven weeks. Instruction begins in the classroom before moving into the water. The candidates learn emergency procedures. They study the effects of deep-water diving on the human body and how to survive it. This phase tests the candidates' comfort and their ability to make sound decisions while submerged in deep, dark water.

Third Phase is seven weeks of land warfare training. Candidates practice reading a map and using a compass to get to their targets. Shooting and small-unit tactics are also important parts of Third Phase. Candidates work long hours to mimic real-life fieldwork. A candidate who finishes Third Phase graduates as a Special Warfare Operator. But he cannot pin the SEAL trident on his uniform yet.

BUD/S candidates practice exchanging dive gear underwater.

SEAL candidates practice marksmanship at Camp Pendleton in California.

During the twenty-six-week SEAL Qualification Training (SQT), candidates master even more SEAL skills. Candidates receive advanced instruction in weapons and explosives. For cold-weather training, they travel to Alaska to learn to operate in the mountains and icy rivers. "Jump School" gives them parachuting skills. Survival, Evasion, Resistance, and Escape School (SERE) prepares future SEALs for the possibility of capture and torture by terrorists and other enemies.

After fifty-nine weeks of training—more than a year—a SEAL candidate earns his trident. Later, SEALs who have completed several combat missions may apply to DEVGRU, or SEAL Team Six. DEVGRU candidates then have to endure Green Team—another nine-month selection process.

Only the best of the best become Navy SEALs.

"My Trident is a symbol of honor and heritage. . . . By wearing the Trident, I accept the responsibility of my chosen profession and way of life. It is a privilege that I must earn every day."

—Navy SEAL Code excerpt

SEAL team membership is not the fast track to promotion. It is not the place to find riches and fame. SEAL teams are special places for special men. Men who will accept any challenge, no matter how difficult. Men measured by the highest standards of military performance.

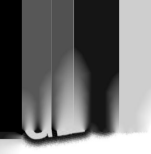

ALLIES
> friendly nations that often
> help one another in wars

AL-QAEDA
> violent terrorist group that
> attacked the United States
> on September 11, 2001

ALTITUDE
> height above the ground or
> water

AMBUSH
> surprise attack from a
> hidden position

ASSAULT
> military attack on enemy
> forces

CHOPPER
> slang term for helicopter

COUNTERTERRORISM
> political or military
> activities designed to stop
> terrorism

DEPLOY
> to send a military unit on a
> mission overseas

EMBASSY
> the official office
> and residence of an
> ambassador in a foreign
> country

ENLISTED
> military members who rank
> below officers

FAST-ROPE
> a special rope, several
> inches thick, used to slide
> down from a helicopter

SUPPRESSOR
> a device attached to a gun
> that muffles the noise so
> when it's fired, instead of
> loud bangs, it sounds like
> snapping fingers

Further Reading

Hamilton, John. *Special Forces*. Edina, MN: ABDO Publishing, 2007.

Lusted, Marcia Amidon. *Marine Force Recon: Elite Operations*. Minneapolis: Lerner Publications Company, 2014.

Sutherland, Adam. *Special Forces*. Minneapolis: Lerner Publications Company, 2012.

Yomtov, Nel. *Navy SEALs in Action*. New York: Bearport Publishing, 2008.

Websites

National Navy UDT-SEAL Museum

http://www.navysealmuseum.com/virtualtour.php

Take a virtual tour at the SEAL museum in Fort Pierce, Florida. See online exhibits showcasing SEAL history and watercraft.

Navy Recruiting

http://www.navy.com/careers/special-operations /seals/?campaign=van_seals

Visit the U.S. Navy's official recruiting website. Learn about SEAL training and what a SEAL's job duties are.

Navy SEALs Training

http://www.sealswcc.com/navy-seals-buds-training-first-phase .aspx

Visit the U.S. Navy SEALs website to watch training videos. Learn what to expect if you want to be a SEAL.

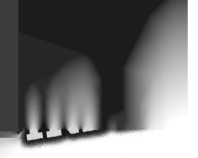

About the Author

Patricia Newman is the author of several books for children, including *Jingle the Brass*, a Junior Library Guild Selection and a Smithsonian-recommended book; and *Nugget on the Flight Deck*, a California Reading Association Eureka! Silver Honor Book for Nonfiction. Watch for *Plastic, Ahoy!* from Millbrook Press in 2014. Visit her at www.patriciamnewman.com.